GROSS STUFF IN YOUR SCHOOL

BY PAM ROSENBERG

ILLUSTRATED BY BEATRIZ HELENA RAMOS

ABOUT THE AUTHOR:

Pam Rosenberg lives in Illinois with a husband, two kids, two cats, a hermit crab, a few bugs, and lots of bacteria and other tiny things she doesn't like to think about.

ABOUT THE ILLUSTRATOR:

Beatriz Helena Ramos is an artist from Venezuela who lives and plays in NYC. She works from her animation studio, Dancing Diablo, where she directs animated spots. Beatriz has illustrated a dozen books and she particularly loves gross stories.

The Child's World

Published by The Child's World®
1980 Lookout Drive • Mankato, MN 56003-1705
800-599-READ • www.childsworld.com

Photos: Lighthunter/Shutterstock.com: 17; mike.irwin/Shutterstock.com: cover; Palex66/Dreamstime.com: 18

ISBN 9781503850248 (Reinforced Library Binding)
ISBN 9781503850729 (Portable Document Format)
ISBN 9781503851481 (Online Multi-user eBook)
LCCN: 2021930078

Printed in the United States of America

TABLE OF CONTENTS

IF YOU'RE LIKE MOST KIDS, YOU PROBABLY SPEND A *LOT* OF TIME AT SCHOOL!

But did you know there are other things spending time in your school? Lots of icky, disgusting, gross things? Grab your backpack and your investigator's hat—we're going inside to find out what's gross at school!

WALKING DOWN THE HALLWAY

You walk in the doors at school and head to your classroom. If you are thirsty, maybe you stop to take a drink from the water fountain. That might not be such a good idea. **One study found that school water fountains were the germiest surfaces in school.** There were 2.7 million **bacteria** cells per inch!

Your next stop is your locker. Open the door and . . . **Phew! What's that smell?** Holding your nose, you look through all the stuff jammed on the shelf and way in the back you find a two-week-old sandwich. The bread is loaded with furry white and green mold. Did you know the mold is a member of the **fungus** kingdom? These little critters digest their food outside their bodies. They send out chemicals called **enzymes** that break down food—like moist bread—and then take the tiny bits of food back into their cells.

How did mold land on your sandwich and start growing? Mold **spores** are everywhere. Millions of mold spores are floating happily through the air in your school. And when these spores land on a moist bit of food, they start to grow and spread out.

Okay, throw away the moldy sandwich and move on. You're at the classroom door. Grab that doorknob and head in. Just don't touch you eyes, nose, or mouth with that hand after you touch that doorknob. **Flu germs can live for up to three days on objects like doorknobs!**

IN THE CLASSROOM

Some of those germs from that doorknob probably came from that classmate three seats over. You know the one—he's been sneezing and blowing his nose for the past couple of days. On a healthy day, his nose, like yours, produces lots of snot. **You swallow more than two cups a day!** But when you have a cold, the snot production goes into high gear. It is one of the ways your body tries to get rid of those nasty cold germs. The **mucus**—that's just a fancy word for snot—traps the germs. Then tiny hairs help move all that germ-infested snot to the back of your nose until you can swallow it. I wonder how many cups of snot your classmate will swallow today.

AhAhAhCHOOO!!!! Take cover—your sick classmate has just let out a sneeze and he didn't cover his mouth and nose. Try not to think about all the tiny droplets of mucus that have just been shot out of his nose at a speed of **60 miles per hour (97 kilometers per hour) or more**. Germ-infested mucus traveling as fast as a car on a highway might just be enough to really gross you out!

Everybody settles in and your teacher assigns some pages to read. For a minute it is so quiet you can hear a pin drop. Suddenly, you hear a noise. Then you smell something. Oh no, you bet that Joey ate beans again for dinner and he passed gas. But don't be too quick to blame Joey. It could be any one of your classmates—even your teacher. Did you know that the **average person passes gas about fourteen times a day?**

You finished your assignment before the rest of the class. So you get up to check out the class pet—Hammy the Hamster. He is chewing on something. Come to think of it, he's always chewing on something. Why? Hamsters are rodents and, like all rodents, **their teeth never stop growing**. If a hamster doesn't chew on hard things, its teeth will get too long. Then the teeth can puncture the hamster's jaw or mouth. Ouch!

LUNCHTIME!

Remember that study we mentioned before? The one about how many germs are on different surfaces in schools? Try not to think about this fact when you grab your cafeteria tray: The study results showed that there were **10 times more germs on cafeteria trays than there were on toilet seats!**

Still feeling hungry? Then grab some grub. Eating foods with lots of fiber will fill you up and help keep you from getting hungry before the school day is over. So load up on apples, broccoli, whole wheat bread, and beans. But look out—when all that **fiber** hits your intestines, the bacteria in your body will go to work breaking the fiber down. **And a side product of all that activity is gas.** And your body is going to need to get rid of that gas. So, your classroom might be a very smelly place in the afternoon if everyone eats lots of healthy fruits and veggies!

You sit down at the cafeteria table. Before lunch you washed your hands to make sure they were nice and clean—no germs, nothing to make you sick. So you reach down, grab your sandwich, and take a big bite. Yummy! Maybe now isn't the time to mention that **your mouth is the germiest part of your body.** More than 100,000,000 microscopic critters live there—all kinds of bacteria, fungi, and **viruses**. But don't panic, most of them aren't harmful. Unless you think about them too much, gross yourself out, and end up puking!

If you manage to eat your lunch without thinking about all those bacteria in your mouth, you'll swallow your food. It will travel down a tube called the **esophagus** and into your stomach. In your stomach it will mix with **acid**. The acid helps break the food down into tiny bits that can be absorbed and used by your body. The acid will probably kill off any bacteria you happened to swallow with your food. After all, **the kind of acid that's in your stomach can burn holes in metal!** Why doesn't it burn through your stomach? You know that gloppy goo that drips out of your nose, otherwise known as mucus? Your stomach is lined with mucus too!

BATHROOM BREAK

After eating lunch, you may need to stop in the bathroom. Remember, we already learned that the toilet seat probably has fewer germs than a cafeteria tray. Maybe that is because **fresh pee is cleaner than the spit in your mouth.** It's even cleaner than the skin on your face!

Eeew! Somebody forgot to flush! Disgusting. But now you're thinking, "**Why is poop brown?** Why isn't it the color of the food you eat?" Good question. The brown color in poop comes from **bile**, something your body produces to help break down your food. Bile is made in your liver and it breaks down fats in your food. It is kind of a yellow-green-brown color and that is why your poop is, well, poop-colored. Should you panic if your poop comes out bright green or blue one day? Not if you ate a lot of bright blue or green fruit snacks or other food with food dye in it within the last day or two. All of that food coloring can turn your poop some strange colors!

GYM CLASS

Run a few laps, dodge a few balls, shoot a few hoops, and it all adds up to one sweaty bunch of kids. **Where does all that sweat come from? Glands** in the bottom layer of your skin send out the watery mixture to help your body cool down. Did you ever taste your sweat? If you did, you know that while sweat might be mostly water, it also contains salt. What you might not know is that it contains **urea**, a waste product produced when your body breaks down protein. You know what else contains urea? If you guessed urine, you're correct. Think about that the next time some of your sweat drips down your face and into your mouth!

The palms of your hands may be the sweatiest part of your body, but your feet come in a close second. There are lots of sweat glands in each of your feet. During gym class, your feet are covered in socks and your favorite pair of athletic shoes. Nice and warm . . . and sweating like crazy. Do you know what likes to live in those warm, moist socks and shoes? Bacteria—lots and lots of them! **All those bacteria create one nasty smell.** You might not want to take off your shoes until you get home. Unless, of course, you think having the nickname "Stinky" would be fun!

BACK TO CLASS

Maybe it was something you ate. Maybe it was running around after eating. Maybe you caught the stomach bug that your little sister had a couple of days ago. Whatever it is, your guts are starting to churn. The muscles in your abdomen are squeezing your stomach. Your stomach squeezes and pushes open the **valve** that leads to your esophagus. All that food you ate a little while ago heads back up toward your mouth. The valve in your throat snaps shut over your windpipe and look out—thar she blows! You've just puked all over the hallway in front of your classroom.

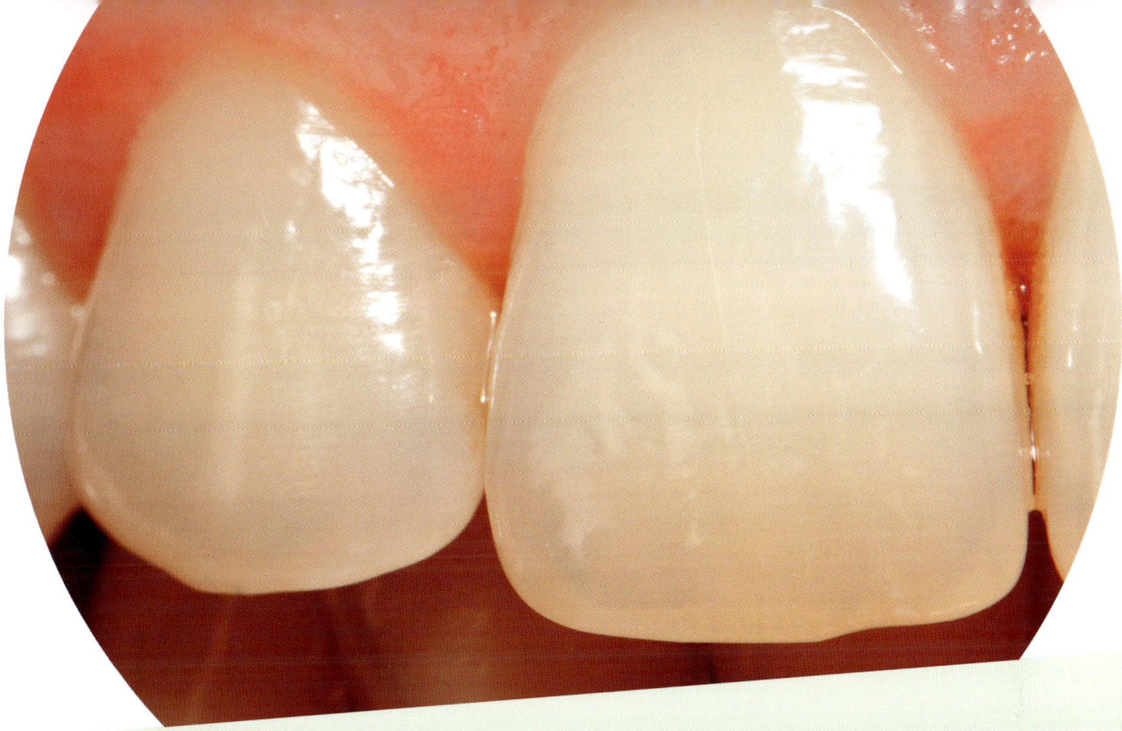

What exactly is that stuff you puked up on the floor? It doesn't look like the food you ate. It's all wet and gooey and it tastes terrible! Remember the stomach acid we talked about earlier? **It sure doesn't taste good!** And if you like having healthy teeth, you'd better head over to a sink and rinse out your mouth. All the acid from the puke can break down the hard covering (called enamel) on your teeth.

THE NURSE'S OFFICE

When your teacher sees what happened, she calls the janitor for a cleanup and sends you to the nurse's office. You head there just in time to find out that one of your classmates has bugs—lice to be exact. Just thinking about it makes your head itch. Every three to six hours, each of those tiny bugs takes a nice drink of blood from your **scalp**. And **when the mom lice aren't eating, they are laying eggs on your hair.** The stuff they use to stick their eggs to hair is like super strong glue. You can wash your hair and brush your hair, but that super strong stuff keeps the egg—called **nits**—attached to your hair. You need to use a special lice-killing shampoo. Then someone has to spend hours combing through your hair with a comb that has lots of teeth that are very close together.

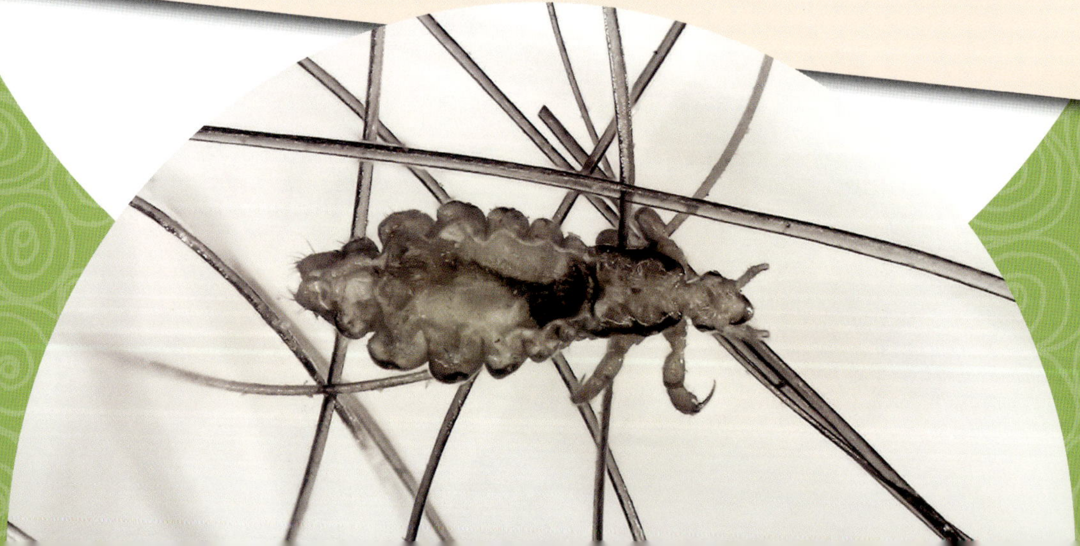

How do those lice get from one head to another? Did you ever borrow someone else's comb? Wear somebody else's hat or scarf? If that kid has lice, chances are you do too after wearing his clothes or sharing his comb!

HOME SWEET HOME

After the nurse checks your head and declares you lice-free, she sends you home. You head to your locker to grab your stuff. You open the locker door and, down near the bottom, you see something crawl out. It's moving really fast. **Ugh, it's a cockroach!** Could this day get any worse? These creepy-looking bugs will eat just about anything. Remember that moldy sandwich you found this morning? For a cockroach, that moldy sandwich is a feast. Of course, so is the stinky sweat in your sneakers, glue on paper, and even paint. If they can't find anything else to eat, they'll happily eat each other. Oh, and you'd better hope that cockroach in your locker wasn't a mommy. Female German cockroaches can produce 500,000 babies in a year!

You head out the door and your mom is waiting to drive you home, where you'll be safe from all the grossness of school. Except that the nurse thinks you have the nasty stomach virus your sister had earlier in the week. **And you probably picked that up at home, didn't you?** Makes you wonder what else is lurking in your house, doesn't it? Maybe school isn't so bad, after all . . . .

GLOSSARY

acid (ASS-id) An acid is a substance that will react with a base to form a salt. Acid in your stomach helps you digest your food.

bacteria (bak-TEER-ee-uh) Bacteria are microscopic living things. Many kinds of bacteria live in your mouth.

bile (BILE) Bile is a liquid made in the liver that helps digest food. Bile helps break down fat in the food you eat and is what gives poop its brown color.

enamel (ih-NAM-uhl) Enamel is the hard, white substance on the surface of your teeth. The acid in vomit can damage the enamel on your teeth.

enzymes (EN-zymz) Enzymes are substances that cause chemical reactions to occur. Molds use enzymes to break down food outside their cells.

esophagus (ih-SOF-uh-guhss) The esophagus is the tube that carries food from the throat to the stomach. When you swallow food, it travels through your esophagus to reach your stomach.

fiber (FYE-bur) Fiber is the part of foods such as fruits and vegetables that passes through your body but doesn't get digested. Eating foods with lots of fiber will fill you up and help keep you from getting hungry before the school day is over.

fungus (FUN-guss) A fungus is a living organism that reproduces by creating spores. Mold is a member of the fungus kingdom.

glands (GLANDZ) Glands are organs in the body that produce chemicals or help chemicals leave the body. Glands in the bottom layer of your skin called sweat glands send out sweat to help your body cool down.

mucus (MYOO-kuss) Mucus is the sticky liquid that lines the inside of your nose, throat, mouth and some other body parts. The mucus in your nose helps trap germs and dirt.

nits (NITS) Nits are eggs that are laid by lice. Lice attach nits to human hair with a substance that acts as a strong glue.

rodents (ROHD-uhnts) Rodents are mammals with large, sharp front teeth that keep growing. Rodents have to gnaw on hard objects to keep their teeth from growing too long. Hamsters are rodents.

scalp (SKALP) Your scalp is the skin that covers the top of your head. Lice survive by drinking blood from human scalps.

spores (SPORZ) Spores are reproductive cells of fungi and plants. When mold spores land on moist food, they begin to grow.

urea (yoo-REE-uh) Urea is a waste product formed when the body breaks down protein. Sweat and urine both contain urea.

valve (VALV) A valve is a movable part that controls the flow of a liquid or gas through an opening. When you throw up, the valve that covers the opening to your windpipe closes so that vomit doesn't get into your lungs.

viruses (VY-ruhss-ez) Viruses are living things that are smaller than bacteria and cause diseases. Many kinds of viruses, bacteria, and fungi live in your mouth.

FOR MORE INFORMATION

Hirschmann, Kris. *The Sticky, Stinky Science Book.* Lake Forest, CA: QEB Publishing, 2018.

Mould, Steve. *The Bacteria Book: The Big World of Really Tiny Microbes.* New York, NY: DK Publishing, 2018.

National Geographic Kids. *Weird But True! Gross: 300 Slimy, Sticky, and Smelly Facts.* Washington, DC: National Geographic Kids, 2016.

Visit our website to learn more about gross stuff in your school:
childsworld.com/links

Note to Parents, Teachers, and Librarians: We routinely verify our weblinks to make sure they are safe, active sites—so encourage your readers to check them out!

INDEX